Happy Land

Kim Baker

Spotty Flamingo

Happy Land

ISBN: 978-1-9998486-2-0

Cover photographs by Kim Baker, 2019.

All black and white photographs courtesy of the Baker family.

Inside back cover photograph by Kim Baker, 2019.

First published in the UK 2020 by
Spotty Flamingo Publishing
8 Milton Grove,
Bisley Old Road,
Stroud,
Gloucestershire
GL5 1NP
An imprint of Tracy Spiers illustration
www.tracyspiers.co.uk

Text printed on 100% recycled paper at **MDL Kelex Ltd**
Unit 16, Stroudwater Business Park,
Stonehouse,
Gloucestershire
GL10 3SX
sales@mdlkelex.co.uk
01453 791400

Other Publications

The Lavinia Tree by Kim Baker
Published by Chrysalis Poetry, 2017.

For my Dad,
Robert Bruce Baker.

To Lionel and Val,

with love
from
Kim

X

thekimbaker@hotmail.com

Contents

Happy Land

The Bakers and Miles lived on Avenue Terrace
along with the Shills, Boxes and Lewis.
All family, congregated together as
swifts on one long row of red brick.
Cyril Fenner was born at number sixteen,
then brought his bride Lilla to thirty-two.
Both his sons were born upstairs,
sharing the attic till leaving home.
The eldest son Terry, newly married to Iris,
resided at Granno Shill's in forty-two,
then when she passed they bought her house
where Julie and Bev spent their early years.
At number nine was Auntie Agg,
at fourteen her sister Ida and husband Arthur.
At ten Kitty Box ran the shop from her front room.
More cousins completed this family tree,
not many spaces left to occupy the street.
At one time, the forty-four homes housed
twenty people all related to me.
Built in 1890 on Everland Field, this row
affectionately known as Happy Land.

In Your Time

I was your constant companion,
went everywhere with you.

Shared all your waking hours,
enjoyed the continual motion,
hustle and bustle of home.

Sometimes you would let me sit
and watch you bake, as you dipped
your fingers to wrists in the bowl.

I adorned your evenings,
flashed gold with pride in the light.
How I loved you staring at my face.

At bedtime you stretched me out,
gently resting my head.

We were connected, you and I.
In sync with each other.

I died with you, but live on.
I sit now in a similar room,
motionless, speechless. Hands tied.

Paper Boy

Rob started the round when he were twelve.
For five years, at half past six, I brought him up tea and toast.
He'd ride to Eastington where I'd gone to school,
to deliver papers from Spring Hill Pitch
to Walt Miles, his mum's cousins house by Pike Bridge,
across the track to Oldbury House;
the school for naughty girls.
With his wages he saved up
enough to buy a record player,
soon there was vinyl an' all.
I couldn't abide Rudy's Rock, that had to go back.
I weren't one bit impressed with Rock n' Roll.
I never swore in front of my son,
but once when he were nine
we was walking up Devereaux
he said, *I can't walk up this bloody hill.*
Lilla stared in shock
what did you say our Robert? Cyril....!
It was my job to take him aside, whisper in his ear
that kind of language is not to be used again.
I may have threatened to hit him, but I never did.
Not our way. If he were naughty
in the cupboard he went, under the stairs
to stay in the pantry 'til he said sorry.
He's turned out well. He's walking out with a lovely girl, Jan,
soon to be happily settled, as our Terry is with Iris.

Eleanor Miles

Entirely out of my own head, it read,
alongside a drawing of a hair pin,
was how you signed my autograph book.
More precious than any famous person's words.
I hated my freckles. You said
it's where the sun has kissed you.
Uncomfortably taller than my elder sister
you encouraged me *little is good, but big is better.*
When seated you always looked so
excited, your legs shook with it.
You never married but shared a husband?
No children. The church family I envied,
always visiting, caring, bringing flowers.
My priority on arrival was to play
with Jackie Jones, yellow Labrador Retriever,
really your nightdress holder.
You joked you would leave him
to me in your will. There was no need,
when the time came it was unquestionable.
After Granny died, I dreaded whom of my
aunts and uncles would be next.
I admired the way you weren't afraid of death.
After the stroke, I saw you in hospital
asleep in a coma, curled up, childlike.
A friend said I had to let you go.
That night I prayed to God, He could have you.
The morning came with a phone call.
I was asked to wear your robes,
take your seat in the choir stalls.
I knew your coffin held only a frame,
your presence so strong beside me.
You gave me faith, joy and song.
Over thirty years on, Jackie Jones
still lies at the end of my bed,
with the slightest smell of you,
my inimitable Great-Auntie Nell.

Not Out

One minute I'm sorting through boxes
the next I'm bowled over.
I sit down on the bed.
I've found Dad's bat in the attic
with a pair of wicket keepers gloves.
He had such large hands,
bigger than mine, he was taller too,
over six foot. Mum said
he was one of Pharaoh's lean kind.
He taught me to play in the back yard,
we'd bowl down the alley to the tin fence.
Fred in callipers next door loved to play.
When neighbours complained of the din
Dad would remind them how good it was for Fred.
Sometimes Dad parked Gandhi outside the house at night
the lorry was ideal for rolling over the grass verge.
The next day we'd wake up to find our own pitch,
set up the wicket, take it turns to bat and bowl;
hours of fun playing lay-by cricket.
I smile, take off the gloves. Time for tea.

Jackie Jones

Memories stuffed into seams,
fur-lined dreams while you slept.
I was kept on the edge,
the eiderdown padded my paws,
waiting for you to rise from slumber.

Once a week a girl came to visit,
straight up the stairs she'd come to find me,
bring me down to play in the front room.
Ignoring all others, devoted her time to adore me.
You said you'd leave me to her in your will.

Forty years on, I've faded, gathered some dust,
yet this grown up girl keeps loving me.
I lie at her feet, a sleeping dog, still
content with daily fuss as she makes the bed,
but she'll never know why I'm called Jackie Jones.

Nine Lives

A miracle of wartime
to a middle aged lady wheelchair bound.
In the dark that she was pregnant,
gave birth to a child
lighter than a bag of sugar,
weighing only three pounds.
The vicar was summoned
that night to read the last rites.

While children were evacuated elsewhere,
Stonehouse was considered safe
and yet, behind your house
loomed Hoffmans factory,
making parts for aeroplanes.
After the war, maps by the Jerries
were found earmarking this site.
You escaped planned bombing.

You are like Sam the cat with nine lives.
Escaping death as if you are immortal.
Every holiday with you brought different dangers.
Once putting your hand through glass in the lift,
or walking out onto the balcony
head first through the window;
they use stickers now to warn people.
Or trapping your finger in the bed frame.

More serious, surviving a gas explosion
with your head inside the boiler,
you singed hair off your hands and eyebrows
but not a single burn to your face.
Worse of all, peritonitis, that emergency operation,
and another having part of your stomach removed.
You are a wonder Dad how you sail through
each disaster and live to tell the tale.

The Blade

I remember the paper knife.
It sliced my heart out.
That letter tore our life apart
took my smile away forever.
I dress in black every morning.
I never say your names aloud
but I will not forget you.
Residing in the cottage next to the Spa
time stands still for me.
I have no joy in living
yet, here I am breathing
going about the chores,
cleaning, baking, feeding the geese.
Sitting on the step I sharpen the blade
of the bread knife. What a waste of life.
Albert, my first born, a soldier,
quick to answer the call of duty
first man in Stonehouse to fall.
Fred was gassed and never the same.
Alex, I thought safe, died from his wounds
the day after Armistice -
last man in Stonehouse to pass over.
Poor Lottie left behind,
never to enjoy marriage or carry his child.
My husband Eli hid his pain. We all did.
A knife again, took blood, sliced his throat
but cruelly left him alive, for shame.
The court found him guilty but spared him jail.
His next attempt could not fail.
I am grateful to the coroner
leaving out the cause of death.
The only light in my life is little Rob
he reminds me of my boys.
He comes to call once a fortnight.
I fatten him up with cold potatoes and butter.

My hand shakes as I use the knife.
There's always treacle tart to follow.
We have an understanding, Rob and I.
He knows while Grandma will not smile
behind this dour face
lies a mother's love,
never forgotten.

Class

Too early for a Saturday we climb in,
sit back on cream leather seats yawning,
hair greased back, all slick and pinned.
The dashboard shines a wooden opulence
triumphantly against the baby blue interior.
I pull down strands of hair to cover my mole.
When we arrive the door creaks wide, a run-down shack,
damp rushes to nostrils, I taste the past.
Costume stuffed rooms meant for changing,
we undress with visible breath.
She greets us warmly, waves her stick.
With glass full in smoke-stained hand,
she puffs and sips, dancing the hour.
Her orange squash smells chemical.
We balance with chair backs. Like her
the barre is just for show, too unstable.
Cobwebs hug the corners,
we cling to the warmth
from the boxy gas heater.
At the end of term she holds parties -
tea and games with rare prizes.
I win a gold bracelet, the clasp is missing.
My sister earns a beautiful tea pot, no handle.
Each week Dad gives our teacher
a lift home after it's over.
She gives us each a fifty pence piece to buy ice-cream.
How I want to be a ballerina like Miss Kay Virgo.

Granny B's

Footsteps echo behind the fireplace
coming nearer, but never seen.
The front parlour's musty smell
all pristine from infrequent use.
The clock ticking away Saturday afternoons.
While Dad dug up spuds
you had forty winks,
I ran down the path
dodging the red ants.
My relief at Grandstand ending
to watch cartoons.
The wooden monkey on the mantelpiece
wanting to take it home.
Hiding from Daleks and wobbling sets,
during endless tea of corned beef, butter, bread,
lettuce and salad cream, home-made cakes.
Guessing the colour of Isla St Clair's dress
from your black and white TV screen,
then rushing home to ours in colour
to see who'd won -
Mum's clever trick to get us home!
The day you said your arm felt numb
I knew I'd never see you again.
I wasn't allowed back in the house
but I remember it all incredibly well,
ten childhood years at Happy Land.

The Spa, Oldends Lane

One of the oldest public houses
in Stonehouse, formed from 16th century cottages.
They used to sell mineral water from the well,
with a pump room, before it just sold beer.
It sat in idyllic surroundings, a farm,
a stream, green fields, with a cottage attached.
The elizabethan grandeur of Oldends Hall nearby
linked to our family through marriage to a Shakespeare.
Eli ran this pub from 1911 with his wife Annie Fenner,
moving in with his five sons and daughter.
When he died their son Fred carried it on.
Cyril and wife Lilla were asked too but declined
so in 1956 it left the Baker family.
Many a celebration was had there even after,
birthday meals and summer evening drinks.
It remained an inn until 2013.
A campaign was run to try to stop the closure
but was sadly unsuccessful.
Now hemmed in by houses and industrial units.
The land once owned by Reginald Baker, his haulage firm
where Cyril, his brother, drove the lorry Gandhi,
including the site of Oldends Hall,
which had been destroyed by fire
was sold to the Milk Marketing Board,
later Dairy Crest and Muller.
It's hard for me to reconcile this dramatic change,
what I see as an eyesore,
as a part of the Baker family history.

Christmas at 32

Christmas morn we open our long stockings,
presents wrapped in paper, devoid of bows.
Every year the men get to frolicking,
in Auntie Nell's stocking - the parson's nose.

Mum and Dad head to Charlie's for a drink.
Auntie Nell downs Harveys Bristol Cream sherry.
Bombs in glass capsules amuse with their stink,
secretly made by Dad and our Terry.

Uncle Bill offers to get in the sheets.
Drunk on rum and black, he takes paraffin
to light the path, soon feels the heat,
sets fire to the washing, there's quite a din!

At Christmas, the time to be decadent,
the Bakers, a place for much merriment.

Party Piece

Games passed down for generations.
Paddy to York was Uncle Bill's favourite,
we played it this Christmas.
Simply slide a ring secretly along string,
while laughter, rhythm of the song
recreates the train chugging along
born from the dawn of rail travel.
I've never had the stomach
for *Nelson's Eye*, whilst blind folded.
I love *Black Magic* with its magic stick.
As a child it took years to work it out
and then I'd forget by the next festive season.
The stick again for more two handed magic
The stick toucheth, one would call to their partner in the other room
let it touch would be the reply, until
On whom does the stick rest? They would always guess right. But how?
I still enjoy this old fashioned fun
pre-dating wireless, television set,
modern technology of telephone or internet.
Drink, food, song and party piece enough.
The Cropthorn Concert Party ran by Auntie May
aided by friends and her sister-in-law, my gran,
as well as Auntie Nell. Dressing up, singing,
performing sketches. They performed all over
as far as Dursley, Avening and even Cirencester.
Even you, Dad, participated as a child,
acting as a ventriloquist's dummy. With mask,
sitting on your cousin Cyril's knee
you fooled them all that you were miming,
no wonder he did so well at not moving his lips..
The sisters Lilla, Nell and Ida as teenagers sang as *The Jesters*
their fame well known at the time. Even your dad was said
to be first to set off the singing on coach trips.
Auntie Nell sang for 60 years in the choir at Leonard Stanley,
Auntie May entertaining *the old fogies* well into her eighties.

The Lone Ranger?

Just rode in from the wild west
of Nupend to Stonehouse.
Dismount the saddle
of Gandhi my ride
stop by the saloon
spitting straw
on the sawdust floor
of the Spa bar.
Everyone freezes,
stares at me.
I watch tumbleweed.
Standing 5 foot tall
at the door
of the O.K. Corral,
hand ever ready
to draw my gun
from the holster,
give it a spin,
pull that trigger.
I'm the Marshall, Wyatt Earp.
A man in chaps
demands
who's that kid?
Granno Shill with apron
leads our little Rob
out by the hand
to take him home.

The Gang

Six kids, Stonehouse residents
in a group playing together.
Brian Butlin, Ron Williams,
Mel Powell and Laurence Duxbury,
myself and just another,
we allowed one girl, Jenny Gingel.
Hide and seek, walking the plank
across the canal, bows and arrows,
hours spent with toy guns as cowboys,
honing cricket skills in the street.
A favourite game was dressing up.
Using old black bags, we cut holes for our heads
immediately transforming us.
All of us want to be Batman,
Jenny can be Robin.

Midwinter's Night

Snow has settled in comfort,
drifts high enough to inspire imagination.
A tar black sky, impossibly dark,
save the polar contrast
of white gleams reflecting light.
Gas lamps inside glow warmth.
One teenage boy braves the night cold.
Lovingly he sculpts a snowman
on top of the frozen water butt.
Our Rob'll love this!
He is proud of his work,
crooked carrot nose,
button brown eyes,
pipe smokes from invisible mouth.
His own scarf wraps the finale.
I must get Rob up. Terry rushes inside,
grabs his Dad's old Home Guard torch
runs two flights to reach the attic.
Come and see what I've made for you!
The pair fly down narrow treads,
a handsome lad, all grown and courting,
followed by a version of himself,
nine years younger.
Their excitement fills three red brick storeys.
Mother and father *must come quick.*
Outside, smiles all round, admiring comments
are quickly silenced,
by a greater wonder -
something bigger, more beautiful, spectactular.
Enlarged pupils stare above the snowman,
beyond the roofs of Hoffmans
at the bottom of the garden,
up higher, to the midwinter skies
strangely ablaze in colour.
Flashes, moving swirls of greens and blues,
mystically dance, charged by nature.

An illumination show of mysterious beauty.
Four faces held in awe, can't believe this is happening.
The spell only broken by excited chatter,
knocking on doors, as neighbours spread the word -
the Northern Lights are performing south
over Stonehouse tonight, one night only.

Picking up Swans

I knew if I said,
tell me about Grandad
it would postpone bedtime.

The man I never knew
who handled a cob
that landed in his garden.

It swooped down one rainy day
mistaking the path for the canal
wingspan of a dragon.

Hissing it's anger,
no one would go near
in fear of bites or broken bones.

But he, calmly walked up,
grabbed his neck,
tucked body under arm

strode past the tattlers,
their mouths agape,
taking him back to water.

I've loved hens, ducks and geese.
Maybe one day I'll be ready
to rescue a swan just like Cyril Fenner.

The Seven Sisters

Their story is like a novel,
but not the series by Lucinda Riley.
Both are tales of love and loss
their constellations crossed
with heartache.

They were all stars in their own right,
but proud to be part of the same tribe.
Miles between them kept them close,
once married, Miles parted them,
except for one.

Eve moved her orbit to Cardiff
with Will Green, made six new stars.
Winn and Jack did the same at Newmarket,
Lilla and Cyril revolved around one son
with a later surprise.

The ancient gods gave gifts
but sometimes took them back.
Mar and Bill lost Colin, aged two, to tuberculosis,
Ida and Arthur lost Barbara, also two, to meningitis.
Their pain united them.

Ag found love in her fifties to Edward,
too late for children.
Nell said all likely suitors were engaged
or married, that she never found
the right one.

These sisters from Seven Waters
also had a brother, Stew, married to Minnie,
he died young, left no offspring. They all
disappeared one by one, as doves,
finally taking their place in the sky.

What's in a Name?

When you were young, you got names mixed up.
Your brother was known as Maxi Baker.
Tim Sims, his best mate, told you
Hey Rob, tell your dad
your Maxi's going out with Iris Hazel.
You, in error, said he was seeing Horace Hazel!

When you went courting some years later
you brought Jan Ham home to meet your parents.
You never warned her your family called you by a different name,
or how there had been two Robert Bakers in your class,
that you became a Bruce instead, or Bob, or Rob,

but what's in a name?

The Ham Baker Alliance

Ham Baker is a household name of stability

You engineered it well, apprentice of Daniels.
Despite your shyness you controlled your nerves,
offered her liquid, asked her to dance
knowing perfectly well this was not your strong point.
Yet in the flow you could do rock n' roll.
Your smart appearance, jet black hair and kind nature
soon won young Janet Ham over. You loved her
from afar for a year, before she knew you existed.
She was quite a catch, all your friends fancied her,
the chic hairdresser from Madame Pompadour's.
Every Sunday you'd watch her leave church
on Bedford Street, Stroud, from the upstairs window
of The Flamingo Grill coffee shop. It took a while for
this machine to stop being idle and get into action.
But once you did, the wheels were in motion
forming a union that deals with precision.
For your first date you took her to the Ritz! (next to Woolworths).
Fifty-six years of marriage, two girls and five grandchildren.
Predicted bliss from the drain covers in the road where you live,
that say **Ham Baker,** an established unity written in history.

The Seamstress

Before my wedding
I dream of you.
We converse on marriage.
You tell me how
you hand stitched
your beautiful dress.
I have not seen you
since I was ten.
I wish you could be there.
The dream's so real
as soon as I awake
I ring my dad.
He tells me
every detail
was true.

Memories Down Lodgemore Lane

I can still smell the smokey tea
made for me by Ken Lusty.
It's the four o'clock break
cups clash on the trolley
beside an industrial tea pot.
His greased black hair distracts me
from the fag in his mouth,
my cup his ashtray.
Men in overalls pour in,
friendly banter ensues,
welcome relief from homework.
My daily routine to walk from school
down Lodgemore Lane to Fromehall Mill,
home to the engineering firm
where my Dad, a draftsman, worked.
I pass the pond, admire ducks and swans,
observe factory workers opposite,
ladies at looms, raising the nap
with teazels by hand.
I remember seeing Fromehall on fire,
flames engulfing the roof, shattering windows
but not penetrating its thick stone walls.
During repairs, the drawing office moved
to the building behind where Stroudwater Red
was made for guards earlier in the century.
On the wall a handwritten message
remember Marion's birthday.
Rolled up like a cigarette in the wall
Dad found a wage slip from '32 belonging to
Marion Savory of Leonard Stanley.
His discovery more special as she was his Aunt..
These memories link me, personally,
to the history of Strachan's textile industry.

Burst

The day my dad's insides burst,
I was happily at home reading a book,
until Mum's words *Dad, ambulance, Gloucester A and E,*
sent shock waves through my nervous system,
drive carefully.
I don't remember getting there,
through the rain, a blur of blades,
Stroud Road nor Eastern Avenue,
just the kind face who ushered me
past queues, through double doors,
to the trolley and a man that resembled my dad -
somewhat older, greyer, obscured by pain.
My expectant sister met us there,
looking pale and faint in her tiny frame.
Amused nurses sent her home
with an excuse of a football up her jumper.
We wheeled with him all the way to theatre.
I knew this was touch and go,
the surgeon's grave face read
either he had no bedside manner or
he was sure Dad's life was in danger.
My father signed his name in morphine
to do whatever; a full exploratory.
My parents became lovers
saying their goodbyes, before an unwilling witness.
He was taken away,
                            we were left in Purgatory -
a bright, clinical cell to wait the night in.
I can't remember what we talked about,
my mother and I, or how we got through
those eternal, small hours apart from praying our hearts out.
The uptight surgeon came in to see us.
Flopping onto a chair, Daddy Longlegs
buckling beneath him, he took off his mask, his hat,
relaxed and smiled,

Silly bugger, his appendix was in the wrong place!
This doctor who saved my dad stared at the floor.
Relief poured from us all making invisible puddles.
On the ward, after, Tractor John of Frocester
said he'd held bets with the other men,
We thought he was a gonner!
Proud of the surgeon's cut from navel to chin, my dad,
brave Robert the Bruce, showed off his warrior scars,
made a speedy recovery, gained back ten years,
outlived those men and made a vow
never to go back there again.

Photographs

Kim Baker has been a professional actor for twenty years. She trained at Birmingham School of Acting. She is addicted to writing poetry in her spare time. This has been a personal experience for her, trying to capture her Dad's memories and lives of family members that she has never met, or of those she remembers, but has not seen for a very long time. It is unusual now for families to spend a whole lifetime on one particular street or in one village. Stonehouse has changed remarkably during her Dad's life and she hopes these poems offer a glimpse of the past.

Acknowledgements

Thank you to my parents for always encouraging me and for a wonderful childhood. Dad, thank you for Basil Rathbone on Friday evenings, Saturdays at Granny B's and our fun Superteams when the lounge became a sports field.

Thank you to Eley for editing support and with my eclectic family (those loved now and always) for a happy space to be creative.

Thank you to my sister, Tracy Spiers, for publishing this book and being a part of this family project. www.tracyspiers.com

Thank you Anna Saunders.
www.cheltenhampoetryfestival.com

Burst first appeared in the **Stroud Poets** series one, pamphlet **no 8** published by Yew Tree Press, 2018.

Memories Down Lodgemore Lane first appeared in **Wool** part of the Stroud Poets series two, pamphlet no 3 published by Yew Tree Press, 2019.

The Blade first appeared as a commended poem in **Graffiti Magazine's** *Silver* Poetry Competition, **issue 25**, 2020.